ADELE 21

ADELE 21

Wise Publications
part of The Music Sales Group

London / New York / Paris / Sydney / Copenhagen / Berlin / Madrid / Hong Kong / Tokyo

PUBLISHED BY
WISE PUBLICATIONS
14-15 BERNERS STREET, LONDON W1T 3LJ, UK.

EXCLUSIVE DISTRIBUTORS:
MUSIC SALES LIMITED
DISTRIBUTION CENTRE, NEWMARKET ROAD,
BURY ST EDMUNDS, SUFFOLK IP33 3YB, UK.

MUSIC SALES PTY LIMITED
20 RESOLUTION DRIVE, CARINGBAH, NSW 2229, AUSTRALIA.

ORDER NO. AM1003123
ISBN: 978-1-78038-021-6
THIS BOOK © COPYRIGHT 2011 WISE PUBLICATIONS,
A DIVISION OF MUSIC SALES LIMITED.

EDITED BY JENNI WHEELER.
MUSIC ARRANGED BY DEREK JONES.
MUSIC PROCESSED BY PAUL EWERS MUSIC DESIGN.

PRINTED IN THE EU.

Rolling In The Deep

Words & Music by Adele Adkins & Paul Epworth

3. Ba - by,___ I_____ have no sto - ry to be told. But I've heard_____ one on you now I'm gon - na make your head burn. Think of___ me_____ in the depths of your des - pair. Make a_____ home down there as mine sure won't be shared.

Drums

D.S. al Coda

9

10

Throw your soul_____ through ev - 'ry o - pen door.

Count your__ bless - ings to find what you look for.

Turn my__ sor - rows in - to trea - sured gold. You'll

pay me__ back in kind and reap just what you've sown._____

13

Turning Tables

Words & Music by Ryan Tedder & Adele Adkins

1. Close e - nough to start a war. All that I

2. Un - der haunt - ed skies I see you. Ooh.

14

your thumb__ I can't breath. So

I won't__ let you__ close e-nough__ to hurt__

__ me. No, I won't res - cue__

you to just__ de-sert__ me. I can't give__ you__ the

18

on my own two feet.

Turn - ing ta - bles.

Rumour Has It

Words & Music by Ryan Tedder & Adele Adkins

You and I have his-to-ry, or don't you re-mem-ber? Sure,_____ she's got it all.__

_____ But ba-by, is that real-ly what you want?_____

𝄋 Dm

Gm⁷

Bless your soul you've got your head in the clouds.__ She's made a fool out-ta you__ and boy she's
𝄋 You've made a fool out-ta me__ so boy I'm

B♭

Dm/A

bring-ing you down.__ She made your____ heart melt, but you're cold to the core.__ Now
bring-ing you down.. You made my____ heart melt, yet I'm cold to the core.__ But

2. She   is half your age   but I'm guess-ing that's the rea-son that you___ strayed.___   I   heard_____ you've been miss - ing me.___   You've been tell-ing peo-ple things you should-n't   be.___   Like when___ we creep   out   when she___ ain't a - round.   Have - n't you   heard   the   ru - mours?

N.C.

D.S. al Coda

23

Don't You Remember

Words & Music by Daniel Wilson & Adele Adkins

-ber_____ me once_ more.

more._____

Gave you the space so you could breath._ I kept my

dis-tance so you would be free._____ In hope that you'd find_ the miss-ing_ piece_ to

bring you back_ to me._____ Why don't you re-

-mem - ber?＿＿＿＿＿＿＿＿＿＿＿＿＿＿＿ Don't you re -

-mem - ber＿＿＿＿＿＿＿＿＿＿＿＿＿＿＿ the rea - son you loved me＿

be - fore? Ba - by, please re-mem - ber me once

more. When will I see you＿ a - gain?＿

31

Set Fire To The Rain

Words & Music by Fraser Smith & Adele Adkins

36

He Won't Go

Words & Music by Paul Epworth & Adele Adkins

Cm   Gm

bear this time,＿ it drags on as I lose my mind.＿ Re-mind-ed by the

Fm

things I find＿ like notes and clothes＿ you left＿ be - hind.＿

Cm   Gm

2. Wake me up,＿ wake me up when all is done.＿ I won't rise un - til this
(4.) voice to - day,＿ I did - n't know a sin - gle word he said.＿ Not one re - sem-blance to the

Fm   Fm⁷ Gm⁷ A♭maj⁷

bat - tle's won.＿ My dig - ni - ty's be - come un - done.} But I won't＿ go.＿
man I met.＿ Just a vague and bro - ken boy in - stead.

Take It All

Words & Music by Adele Adkins & Francis Eg White

48

Lovesong

Words by Robert Smith
Music by Robert Smith, Simon Gallup, Laurence Tolhurst,
Porl Thompson, Boris Williams & Roger O'Donnell

1. When-ev - er I'm___ a - lone___ with you
2. When-ev - er I'm___ a - lone___ with you

you make me feel___ like I am home a - gain.___
you make me feel___ like I am young a - gain.___

When-ev - er I'm___ a - lone___ with you
When-ev - er I'm___ a - lone___ with you

you make me feel___ like I am whole a - gain.___
you make me feel___ like I am fun a - gain.___

How - ev - er far___ a - way,___ I will al -

50

I'll Be Waiting

Words & Music by Adele Adkins & Paul Epworth

1. Hold me clos - er _____ one more time say that you love me _____ in your

wait-ing for___ you___ when you're read-y_____ to love me a-gain.__ I'll put my

hands up. I'll do_____ ev-'ry-thing diff-'rent, I'll be bet-ter to you.__ I'll be___

wait-ing for___ you___ when you're read-y_____ to love me a-gain.__ I'll put my

hands up. I'll___ be___ some-bod-y diff-'rent, I'll be bet-ter to you._____

One And Only

Words & Music by Adele Adkins, Daniel Wilson
& Greg Wells

knows___ why it's tak - en me so long___ to let my doubts_
know___ how it feels to hold you close___ and have you___

go.___ Oh, you're the on - ly one that I want.___ I don't know
tell me which - ev - er road I choose you'll go.___

why I'm scared,_ I've been here be - fore. Ev - 'ry feel - ing, ev - 'ry word,_ I've i - ma -

- gined it all. You'll nev - er know if you nev - er try___ to

for-give your past___ and sim-ply be mine._____ I dare you to___

let me be___ your, your one and on - ly. Prom-ise I'm___

wor - thy to hold in your arms.___ So come on_____ and give___

me the chance___ to prove I am the one who can___ walk that

Someone Like You

Words & Music by Adele Adkins & Daniel Wilson

found a girl___ and you're mar-ried now._____ We were
yes-ter-day___ was the time of our lives._____

I heard___ that your dreams came true. Guess she
born and raised___ in a sum-mer haze. Bound

gave you things___ I did-n't give to you._____ I
by the sur-prise of our glo-ry days.

1° only

Old friend, why are you so___ shy?_ Ain't like

70

3456789

ADELE 21